YOUR KNOWLEDGE HAS VALUE

- We will publish your bachelor's and master's thesis, essays and papers

- Your own eBook and book - sold worldwide in all relevant shops

- Earn money with each sale

Upload your text at www.GRIN.com and publish for free

Bibliographic information published by the German National Library:

The German National Library lists this publication in the National Bibliography; detailed bibliographic data are available on the Internet at http://dnb.dnb.de .

This book is copyright material and must not be copied, reproduced, transferred, distributed, leased, licensed or publicly performed or used in any way except as specifically permitted in writing by the publishers, as allowed under the terms and conditions under which it was purchased or as strictly permitted by applicable copyright law. Any unauthorized distribution or use of this text may be a direct infringement of the author s and publisher s rights and those responsible may be liable in law accordingly.

Imprint:

Copyright © 2016 GRIN Verlag
Print and binding: Books on Demand GmbH, Norderstedt Germany
ISBN: 9783668747968

This book at GRIN:

https://www.grin.com/document/432716

Jennie Robinson

The Efficiency of the Transparency Directive and its Amending Directive 2013/50/EU (TDAD) with the Financial Disclosure Regulation

GRIN Verlag

GRIN - Your knowledge has value

Since its foundation in 1998, GRIN has specialized in publishing academic texts by students, college teachers and other academics as e-book and printed book. The website www.grin.com is an ideal platform for presenting term papers, final papers, scientific essays, dissertations and specialist books.

Visit us on the internet:

http://www.grin.com/

http://www.facebook.com/grincom

http://www.twitter.com/grin_com

Jennie Robinson

Assignment 2

Word count: 2235

Introduction

Public disclosure of some of a company's financial affairs is an important requirement of a limited liability company. In this assignment, we will consider either the Transparency Directive and the Transparency Directive Amending Directive 2013/50/EU (TDAD) of the European Union has proven efficient in setting up the disclosure requirements regarding the financial information and distribution within the European Union, and in keeping with the rationale and objectives of financial disclosure regulation.

Development

Limited Liability Company

According to Sealy & Worthington (2013, p.33), the fundamental result of incorporating limited companies are the company's separate legal personality and its members limited liability. The directors are accountable to deliver the companies' "statutory accounts and reports". Hence the question of reliability and the need of some independent external party to audit the statements and management activities in delivering them (Sealy & Worthington 2013, p.463). According to these authors, this is the ultimate result since "the 'price' that companies must pay for the privileges of incorporation (separate personality) and limited liability is a fair degree of openness and publicity about their affairs". Indeed, they observed that the concept of 'limited' aims suggest the companies resources are not unlimited (Sealy & Worthington 2013, p.715).[1]

Public Disclosure

The idea behind the importance of a limited company's public disclosure of its financial affairs, is to allow the company's investors or creditors "to make an informed judgment about its financial health"(CeFiMS, Unit – p.4)[2]. Public disclosure also aims at motivating the company's good conduct towards requirements and at providing management's positive accountability to the shareholders. The procedure is done through the annual audit of financial statements and their filing at the Companies House (CeFiMS, Unit – p.4)[3]. The Limited Liability Partnership Act was passed in 2000, and set up a

---

[1] Sealy, L. & Worthington S., 2013. *Sealy & Worthington's Cases and Materials in Company Law.* 10th ed., Oxford, Oxford University Press.
[2] Center for Financial and Management Studies, 2016. Legal Aspects of Corporate Finance. 7th revision, London.
[3] Ibid.

new type of legal entity, « a body corporate, with a separate legal personality from that of its members », owing the duty of care to the company (CeFiMS, Unit – p.16)[4]. The auditors' main task is to « conduct an independent professional review of a company's financial statements », that will give reliability (though not guaranteeing correctness) to the concerned investors and creditors (CeFiMS, Unit – p.10). The required Auditor's report, along with the audited financial statements are therefore to ensure the company's statements are in line with the 2006 Companies Act and confirm a good state of the company's affairs (CeFiMS, Unit – p.8). Along with the financial statements, according to the Companies 2006 Act (Section 415) and the EU Accounts Modernisation Directive (2003/51/EEC), the directors' report is required to inform about who are the directors, the amount of dividend they should receive, and the company's business review. (CeFiMS, Unit – p.7). The 2006 Act Section 423 mentions that all these documents need to be presented to the company's shareholders (CeFiMS, Unit – p.9). In addition, changes related to the company's « constitution, directors and share capital, as well as information about their shareholders » are to be notified (CeFiMS, Unit – p.18).[5]

However, the question of the auditors' liability has brought up two conflicting views, whether « it is those who may be affected by their reports who are at risk from financial loss », or it is « the auditors themselves who feel they need their liability to be limited » (CeFiMS, Unit – p.14). By 2016, a new Act (in its Section 534) brought new provisions such as to « limit the amount of liability owed to a company by its auditor in respect of any negligence » (CeFiMS, Unit – p.17). [6]

The goals of the Financial Disclosure Regulation

According to Meier-Schatz (1986, p.219), conventional objectives of financial disclosure regulation used to be "investor protection, market efficiency, and corporate governance, as well as broader public policy considerations". The then EEC attempted to "harmonize the corporate laws of its members" by restricting their corporate information rules, that concerned creditors, the employees, and the general public"[7]. These authors (Meier-Schatz 1986, pp.221-222) argue that although investment protection would deter from fraud on "small and uninformed investors" to a certain extent, "the financial disclosure regulation of new securities issues can reduce although not prevent fraudulent practices

---

4   Center for Financial and Management Studies, 2016. Legal Aspects of Corporate Finance. 7th revision, London.
5   Ibid.
6   Ibid.
7   Meier-Schatz, C., 1986. 'Objectives of Financial Disclosure Regulation'. *Journal of Comparative Business and Capital Market Law 8,* (1986) 219-248 North-Holland.

detrimental to small investors"[8].

The market efficiency purpose is questioned since, as Meier-Schatz argue (1986, p.222) that in "not-organized capital markets, which are still of a major economic significance in European countries, small investors cannot rely on market prices as a device for consumer protection". However, they conclude that "mandatory disclosure rules can supply the capital markets with new information and enhance their allocational efficiency" (Meier-Schatz 1986, p.225).[9]

With regard to corporate governance and disclosure, the same authors argue that the objective is to provide "reliable monitoring of managers in the interest of shareholders"(Meier-Schatz 1986, p.226). In other words, the impact of financial disclosure rules on voting rights benefits the informed shareholders on smarter voting decisions, and is therefore related to "the direct control of management's performance by shareholders" (Meier-Schatz 1986, p.227). A common view in Europe suggests that "mandatory financial statements secure a more responsible and less selfish management", and thereby promoting "management's adherence to its fiduciary duty to shareholders, especially their duty of loyalty" (Meier-Schatz 1986, p.231).[10]

As for wider public disclosure goals, it has been argued that "the general public has a legitimate claim to be informed about large corporations having a manifold impact on the economy and society" Meier-Schatz (1986, p.229). In this context, disclosure rules on the corporation are to provide an information, confidence and control functions. However, questions remain as to what extent does the public opinion influence over the corporations and managers, or what are the "inherent limitations of financial statements for evaluating corporate management" (Meier-Schatz 1986, p.231). The authors concluded that "the public is thus in no better position than shareholders in the detection and prevention of ineffective and questionable practices of management through the reading of financial statements" (Meier-Schatz 1986, p.231).[11] As to informing the creditors, (Meier-Schatz (1986, p.232) argue that "disclosure regulation supplies creditors with information they need to evaluate the debtors' economic situation and and to assess their own risks" . However, they suggest that "a reference to the creditors' demand for disclosure by debtors is irrelevant when a capital market, investor, or shareholder related regulation provides the financial information".[12] Moreover, informing the employees is due to the fact

---

8   Ibid.
9   Meier-Schatz, C., 1986. 'Objectives of Financial Disclosure Regulation'. *Journal of Comparative Business and Capital Market Law 8,* (1986) 219-248 North-Holland.
10   Ibid.
11   Ibid.
12   Ibid.

that the "workers and their representatives have a legitimate claim to be informed about their employers' economic situation"Meier-Schatz (1986, p.233). Such view is arguable because the employees' interests "are protected by the collective bargaining process between unions and employers" and because "there is no compelling reason to prefer employees of enterprises subject to a mandatory information scheme" Meier-Schatz (1986, p.233).[13]

Efficiency of the EU Directives with the rationale and goals of the financial disclosure regulation
With the wider goal of completing a single market for financial services (back in 1999) and applying international accounting standards (2002) on financial reporting, the Transparency Directive (2004/109/EC) want "efficient, transparent and integrated securities markets [to] contribute to a genuine single market in the Community and foster growth and job creation by better allocation of capital and by reducing costs." In this perspective, "the disclosure of accurate, comprehensive and timely information about security issuers builds sustained investor confidence and allows an informed assessment of their business performance and assets". Along with the goals of the financial disclosure regulation, this Directive aims at enhancing "both investor protection and market efficiency". To reach those aims, "security issuers should ensure appropriate transparency for investors through a regular flow of information". The same idea for public information goes for the corporate governance goal, with shareholders or anyone "holding voting rights or financial instruments that result in an entitlement to acquire existing shares with voting rights. [14] Indeed, it has been argued that a company's shareholders are not always truly identified in its members registry.

It is in this perspective, that the Transparency Directive (2004/109/EC) was to amend previous Directives, through different measures in order to "enable both the company and the market to know who has a controlling interest, or who may be in a position to acquire such an interest in the company" (Sealy & Worthington (2013, p.720).[15]

The 2004 and amended 2013 Directives' purpose is "to ensure transparency of information for investors through a regular flow of disclosure of periodic and on-going regulated information and the dissemination of such information to the public". Such regulated information are in the form of

---

13   Meier-Schatz, C., 1986. 'Objectives of Financial Disclosure Regulation'. *Journal of Comparative Business and Capital Market Law 8,* (1986) 219-248 North-Holland.
14   Official Journal of the European Union L 390/38, December 2004. 'Directive 2004/109/EC of the European Parliament and of the Council of Parliament and of The Council'. [online]. Available from :http://eur-lex.europa.eu/legal-content/EN/TXT/PDF/?uri=CELEX:32004L0109&from=EN [Accessed July 2016]
15   Sealy, L. & Worthington S., 2013. *Sealy & Worthington's Cases and Materials in Company Law.* 10th ed., Oxford, Oxford University Press.

financial reports and information on major holdings of voting rights.[16]

However, the Directive 2013/50/EU followed the operation report of the Directive 2004/19/EC, which suggested "the need to provide for the simplification of certain issuer's obligations with a view to making regulated markets more attractive to small and medium-sized issuers raising capital in the Union", the need to "make the obligations applicable to listed small and medium enterprises more proportionate, whilst guaranteeing the same level of investor protection", the need to abolish the publication of interim management statements, an example of "administrative burden" which "discourage long-term investment" due to seeking short-term performance, the need to bring a more efficient transparency regime with regard to the disclosure of corporate ownership.

Moreover, within the context of transparency and investor protection goals, a new measure is to disclose the payments made by some securities issuers to governments on an annual separate report. Among many other suggestions for improving 2004 Directive, is the idea of harmonizing reports through an electronic format, under the supervision of the ESMA.17 The purpose of the European Securities and Markets Authority (ESMA), a European Union financial regulatory institution and European Supervisory Authority, is "to promote the consistent application of the European securities and markets legislation and International Financial Reporting Standards (IFRS), and especially the provisions of the Transparency Directive" through the scrutiny of disclosed company issuers' financial statements. Public disclosure in this context enables "listed companies and their auditors take due account of these areas when preparing and auditing IFRS financial statements". With regard to the application of the Directive and shareholders voting rights notification, the ESMA has issued a standard form to "provide investors with comparable information on major holdings and simplify the process for persons subject to the notification obligation".[18]

Following this development of standardization and transparency, ESMA is supervising the development of the European Single Electronic Reporting Format (ESEF) in order to transfer the annual financial reports into a "single electronic reporting format that will take effect from 1 January 2020".[19]

---

16 https://www.esma.europa.eu/regulation/corporate-disclosure/transparency-directive Transparency Directive
17 Official Journal of the European Union L 294/13, November 2013. 'Directive 2013/50/EU of the European Parliament and of The Council Parliament and The Council of 22 October 2013 amending Directive 2004/109/EC'. [online]. Available from: http://eur-lex.europa.eu/legal-content/EN/TXT/PDF/?uri=CELEX:32013L0050&from=EN [Accessed July 2016].
18 Ibid.
19 https://www.esma.europa.eu/regulation/corporate-disclosure/transparency-directive
    Transparency Directive

An overview of the financial disclosure regulation goals and the 2004 and 2013 Transparency Directives

Goals of the financial disclosure regulation	Transparency Directive 2004/109/EC [20]	(Amended) Transparency Directive 2013/50 EU [21]
<ul><li>Investor protection</li><li>Market efficiency</li><li>Corporate governance</li><li>Public policy considerations</li></ul>	<ul><li>This Transparency Directive's main purpose was to create "a common basis for periodic information, major shareholding notifications and dissemination and storage of regulated information."</li><li>This Directive call for countries in the EU to publish financial information about income during certain periods of the year, and to notify any information regarding ownership of voting rights.</li><li>A concern for the issuers is that "only one home Member State whose rules will be applied irrespective in which Member State the issuer"s securities are admitted to trading on a regulated market".</li><li>The home Member State is "allowed to impose more stringent requirements than those</li></ul>	<ul><li>It seeks to "reduce the administrative burden which weighed on small and medium issuers, in order to improve their access to capital";</li><li>It aims at more efficient transparency system, especially in the context of publishing information regarding "corporate ownership".</li><li>It requires for periodic information about the state of finance of "the issuer of securities and that of the enterprises it controls".</li><li>Any new distribution of voting rights, the shareholder's identification, the date the change took place and "the threshold of votes reached" must be notified in such a situation: "when a shareholder acquires or yields the shares of an issuer whose shares are admitted for negation on a regulated market and</li></ul>

---

[20] European Securities and Markets Authorities, 2012. 'Transparency Directive (2004/109/EC)' [online]. Available from: https://www.esma.europa.eu/sites/default/files/library/2015/11/2012-198.pdf
[21] Official Journal of the European Union L 294/13, November 2013. 'Directive 2013/50/EU of the European Parliament and of The Council Parliament and The Council of 22 October 2013 amending Directive 2004/109/EC'. [online]. Available from: http://eur-lex.europa.eu/legal-content/EN/TXT/PDF/?uri=CELEX:32013L0050&from=EN [Accessed July 2016].

laid out in the TD". • Transparency is required from issuers who are admitted to trade securities on a regulated market. • This Directive's objective is to provide more information to investors about those same issuers that have presence (location or operation) within the European Union.	which carry voting rights, s/he must notify the issuer of the percentage of voting rights that s/he possesses following the operation". • A new measure in this Directive concerns the annual report of payments to the local government made by listed companies in the sectors of oil, gas and minerals, and forest farming.

Conclusion

In view of the above, the Transparency Directives have been great steps towards bringing more transparency, while pursuing the wider goal of a single market for financial services with a European Single Electronic Reporting Format to transfer the annual finanical reports. The Directives as with other EU developments and reports, are remained open for improvements, and thereby showing flexibility in following its goals. The Directives have provisions on breaches and for EU Member States to apply sanctions and administrative measures. The Directives have been effective in establishing minimum requirements regarding the financial information and distribution all over the European Union, in keeping with the rationale and objectives of financial disclosure regulation

References

Bank Reserve. [online]. Available from: http://www.investopedia.com/terms/b/bank-reserve.asp [Accessed May 2016].

Center for Financial and Management Studies, 2016. Legal Aspects of Corporate Finance. 7th revision, London.

European Securities and Markets Authorities, 2012. 'Transparency Directive (2004/109/EC)' [online]. Available from: https://www.esma.europa.eu/sites/default/files/library/2015/11/2012-198.pdf

Issuers of securities - more transparent information : Summary of Directive 2004/109/EC – Transparency requirements in relation to information about issuers whose securities are admitted to trading on a regulated market. [online] Available from :http://eur-lex.europa.eu/legal-content/EN/TXT/?uri=URISERV:l22022 [Accessed July 2016].

Koch & MacDonald, 2015. *Bank Management.* Eighth ed. Boston, MA, USA: Cengage Learning.

Meier-Schatz, C., 1986. 'Objectives of Financial Disclosure Regulation'. *Journal of Comparative Business and Capital Market Law 8,* (1986) 219-248 North-Holland.

Official Journal of the European Union L 294/13, November 2013. 'Directive 2013/50/EU of the European Parliament and of The Council Parliament and The Council of 22 October 2013 amending Directive 2004/109/EC'. [online]. Available from: http://eur-lex.europa.eu/legal-content/EN/TXT/PDF/?uri=CELEX:32013L0050&from=EN [Accessed July 2016].

Official Journal of the European Union L 390/38, December 2004. 'Directive 2004/109/EC of the European Parliament and of the Council of Parliament and of The Council'. [online]. Available from :http://eur-lex.europa.eu/legal-content/EN/TXT/PDF/?uri=CELEX:32004L0109&from=EN [Accessed July 2016]

Regulatory Alert, February 2016. 'Disclosure Obligation Following Implementation Of The Amended Transparency Directive'. [online]. Available from: https://www.stibbe.com/en/news/2016/february/regulatory-alert-february-2016 [Accessed July 2016].

Sealy, L. & Worthington S., 2013. *Sealy & Worthington's Cases and Materials in Company Law.* 10th ed., Oxford, Oxford University Press.

YOUR KNOWLEDGE HAS VALUE

- We will publish your bachelor's and master's thesis, essays and papers

- Your own eBook and book - sold worldwide in all relevant shops

- Earn money with each sale

Upload your text at www.GRIN.com
and publish for free